So Precious

Ma. Elvira Estrada

Published by Ma. Elvira Estrada, 2024.

While every precaution has been taken in the preparation of this book, the publisher assumes no responsibility for errors or omissions, or for damages resulting from the use of the information contained herein.

SO PRECIOUS

First edition. May 23, 2024.

Copyright © 2024 Ma. Elvira Estrada.

ISBN: 979-8224666171

Written by Ma. Elvira Estrada.

Table of Contents

Chapter 1:
Introduction to Value and Worth
The Concept of Preciousness

The concept of preciousness goes beyond mere monetary value; it encompasses the intrinsic worth and significance that an object or entity holds. Preciousness can be subjective, varying from person to person based on their personal experiences, emotions, and cultural background.

One aspect of preciousness is sentimental value. Objects or memories that hold sentimental value are often considered precious because they evoke strong emotions and memories tied to them. For example, a family heirloom passed down through generations may not have significant monetary value but holds immense sentimental worth due to its connection to one's heritage and ancestors.

Another dimension of preciousness is rarity. Items that are rare or unique are often deemed precious because of their scarcity. This rarity can be natural, such as a rare gemstone or a limited edition collectible, or it can be artificially created through deliberate actions like limited production runs.

Cultural significance also plays a crucial role in determining the preciousness of an object. Certain artifacts or symbols may hold immense value within a specific culture or community, making them highly prized and revered. These objects become repositories of history, tradition, and identity, further enhancing their preciousness.

Moreover, the concept of preciousness extends beyond material possessions to intangible qualities like time, relationships, and experiences. Moments shared with loved ones, acts of kindness, and personal achievements can all be considered precious due to their impact on our lives and well-being.

In essence, the concept of preciousness is multifaceted and deeply intertwined with human emotions, perceptions, and values. Understanding what makes something precious allows us to appreciate the richness and diversity of our world beyond mere material wealth.

Understanding Value in Our Lives

Value in our lives extends far beyond mere material possessions or monetary worth. It encompasses the intrinsic significance and impact that various aspects hold on our well-being, relationships, and overall sense of fulfillment. Understanding value in our lives allows us to appreciate the richness and diversity of experiences that shape who we are.

One crucial aspect of value is the importance of time. Time is a finite resource that we all possess, and how we choose to spend it reflects our priorities and values. Moments shared with loved ones, pursuing passions, or engaging in activities that bring joy can be considered invaluable due to the positive impact they have on our emotional well-being.

Furthermore, relationships play a significant role in determining value in our lives. The connections we form with others, whether family, friends, or colleagues, contribute to our sense of belonging and support network. These relationships provide emotional nourishment, companionship, and a sense of community that adds immense value to our lives.

Personal growth and self-improvement also hold great value in shaping who we are as individuals. Setting goals, overcoming challenges, and achieving personal milestones contribute to a sense of accomplishment and self-worth. These experiences not only enhance our skills and knowledge but also boost our confidence and resilience.

In essence, understanding value in our lives requires us to look beyond material possessions and external markers of success. It involves recognizing the intangible qualities like time spent meaningfully, relationships nurtured with care, and personal growth achieved through perseverance. By acknowledging these aspects of value, we can cultivate a deeper appreciation for the richness and complexity of human existence.

Exploring the Factors that Determine Worth

Understanding the factors that determine worth is essential in recognizing the multifaceted nature of value in our lives. While value encompasses various aspects like time, relationships, and personal growth, worth delves deeper into the specific elements that contribute to our sense of self-worth and fulfillment.

One crucial factor that determines worth is authenticity. Being true to oneself and aligning actions with values and beliefs adds intrinsic value to our experiences. Authenticity fosters a sense of integrity and self-respect, enhancing our overall worth by staying true to who we are at our core.

Another significant factor influencing worth is resilience. The ability to bounce back from setbacks, face challenges head-on, and adapt to changing circumstances showcases inner strength and determination. Resilience not only enhances our self-worth but also empowers us to navigate life's uncertainties with confidence and grace.

Furthermore, empathy plays a vital role in determining worth. The capacity to understand and connect with others on an emotional level fosters meaningful relationships and a sense of belonging. Empathy enriches our interactions with compassion and understanding, elevating our worth through genuine connections with those around us.

In addition, self-awareness is a key factor in determining worth. Understanding one's strengths, weaknesses, values, and motivations allows for personal growth and development. Self-awareness enables individuals to make informed decisions aligned with their authentic selves, ultimately contributing to a greater sense of worth and fulfillment.

In essence, exploring the factors that determine worth involves delving into the core aspects that shape our identity, values, and relationships. By recognizing authenticity, resilience, empathy, and self-awareness as key influencers of worth, individuals can cultivate a deeper appreciation for their intrinsic value and lead more fulfilling lives.

Chapter 2:
Assigning Value to Objects

Sentimental attachments to material possessions

Sentimental attachments to material possessions play a significant role in shaping our perceptions of value and worth. These emotional connections go beyond the physical attributes of an object, encompassing personal memories, experiences, and relationships that are intertwined with it.

One key aspect of sentimental attachments is the nostalgia they evoke. Objects that hold sentimental value often serve as tangible reminders of past events or loved ones, triggering emotions and memories associated with those moments. For example, a childhood toy may hold sentimental value not because of its monetary worth but because it represents innocence, joy, and comfort from earlier years.

Moreover, sentimental attachments can also be tied to cultural heritage and family traditions. Items passed down through generations carry the weight of history and ancestry, connecting individuals to their roots and identity. Family heirlooms like jewelry, furniture, or photographs become cherished possessions due to their role in preserving familial stories and legacies.

In addition to personal significance, sentimental attachments can provide a sense of continuity and belonging. Objects that have been part of one's life for an extended period can offer stability and comfort in times of change or uncertainty. They act as anchors to one's past self, grounding individuals in their journey through life.

Furthermore, sentimental attachments can foster bonds between individuals through shared experiences and memories associated with specific objects. Family members or friends may bond over common items that hold sentimental value for all parties involved, strengthening relationships and creating lasting connections based on shared history.

In essence, understanding the depth of sentimental attachments to material possessions allows us to appreciate the emotional richness they bring into our lives. These objects serve as conduits for memories, emotions, and relationships that shape our sense of identity and connection to others.

The Role of Rarity and Scarcity in Valuing Objects

Rarity and scarcity play a crucial role in determining the value of objects, both in terms of monetary worth and emotional significance. When an object is rare or scarce, it automatically becomes more desirable due to its limited availability. This exclusivity creates a sense of uniqueness and prestige that can elevate the perceived value of the object.

Objects that are rare often hold a special allure for collectors and enthusiasts who seek to acquire unique pieces that set them apart from others. Whether it's a limited edition artwork, a vintage car model, or a rare stamp, the scarcity of these items adds to their appeal and drives up their market value.

Furthermore, rarity can also enhance the sentimental value of an object. When something is hard to come by, it becomes more precious to its owner, creating a deeper emotional attachment based on its uniqueness. Family heirlooms that are passed down through generations gain additional significance when they are one-of-a-kind pieces with historical importance.

In some cases, scarcity can lead to competition among individuals vying for the same coveted item, further driving up its perceived value. Auctions for rare collectibles often see intense bidding wars as passionate collectors compete to own a piece of history or a highly sought-after artifact.

Understanding the role of rarity and scarcity in valuing objects allows us to appreciate how these factors contribute to shaping our perceptions of worth and desirability. Whether it's an antique treasure or a modern-day rarity, the limited availability of certain objects adds layers of complexity to their valuation, making them prized possessions sought after by many.

Cultural and Historical Significance of Certain Objects

Cultural and historical significance play a vital role in assigning value to objects beyond their rarity or scarcity. Objects that have a rich cultural or historical background often hold immense importance due to the stories they carry and the connections they represent.

For example, artifacts from ancient civilizations such as Egyptian hieroglyphics or Greek pottery are not only rare but also culturally significant. These objects provide insights into the beliefs, practices, and daily lives of past societies, making them invaluable in understanding human history.

In addition, objects associated with significant historical events or figures gain added value due to their connection to pivotal moments in time. For instance, a sword wielded by a famous warrior or a dress worn by a renowned leader becomes more than just an object; it becomes a tangible link to the past that holds immense historical significance.

Cultural artifacts like traditional clothing, religious symbols, or ceremonial objects also hold deep cultural meaning for communities around the world. These objects are not merely items of material value but embodiments of cultural identity and heritage that are passed down through generations.

Furthermore, certain objects may symbolize important milestones or achievements in human history, such as the first moon landing or the discovery of penicillin. These items become iconic representations of human ingenuity and progress, transcending their physical form to embody larger narratives of innovation and advancement.

Understanding the cultural and historical significance of certain objects allows us to appreciate them not just as commodities but as repositories of knowledge, memory, and identity. By recognizing the stories embedded within these objects, we can gain a deeper understanding of our shared human experience and the diverse tapestry of cultures that shape our world.

Chapter 3:
Valuing Relationships

The Importance of Emotional Connections

Emotional connections play a crucial role in valuing relationships, objects, and experiences. These connections go beyond mere sentimentality; they shape our perceptions of worth and contribute to our sense of identity and belonging.

One key aspect of emotional connections is the depth of personal memories and experiences intertwined with an object or relationship. These emotional ties evoke nostalgia, triggering feelings of joy, comfort, or even sadness associated with past events. For example, a family heirloom may hold sentimental value not just because it is rare but because it symbolizes the love and history shared among generations.

Moreover, emotional connections foster bonds between individuals through shared experiences and memories. Objects that hold sentimental value can serve as conversation starters or reminders of cherished moments, strengthening relationships and creating lasting connections based on mutual understanding and empathy.

In addition to personal significance, emotional connections provide a sense of continuity and stability in times of change or uncertainty. Objects that carry emotional weight act as anchors to one's past self, grounding individuals in their journey through life and providing a sense of comfort and familiarity.

Furthermore, understanding the importance of emotional connections allows us to appreciate the richness they bring into our lives. Whether it's a childhood toy that represents innocence or a photograph that captures a special moment, these objects serve as conduits for emotions and memories that shape our sense of self and connection to others.

In essence, valuing emotional connections goes beyond material possessions; it encompasses the intangible aspects of human experience that enrich our lives and deepen our relationships with others. By recognizing the significance of these emotional ties, we can cultivate stronger bonds with loved ones and create meaningful connections that transcend time and space.

Nurturing Meaningful Relationships

Nurturing meaningful relationships is essential for fostering emotional connections and building strong bonds with others. It involves investing time, effort, and genuine care into cultivating relationships that go beyond surface-level interactions.

One key aspect of nurturing meaningful relationships is active listening. By truly listening to others without judgment or distraction, we show that we value their thoughts, feelings, and experiences. This practice fosters trust and understanding, laying the foundation for deeper connections based on mutual respect and empathy.

Another important element in nurturing meaningful relationships is communication. Open and honest communication allows individuals to express their thoughts and emotions freely, creating a safe space for vulnerability and authenticity. By sharing openly with one another, people can strengthen their bond and develop a deeper sense of connection.

In addition to communication, showing appreciation and gratitude plays a significant role in nurturing meaningful relationships. Expressing gratitude for the presence of loved ones in our lives or acknowledging their efforts and support reinforces the value we place on these relationships. Small gestures of appreciation can go a long way in strengthening bonds and creating lasting connections.

Furthermore, engaging in shared activities or experiences can deepen the connection between individuals. Whether it's participating in hobbies together, exploring new places, or simply spending quality time with loved ones, shared experiences create memories that strengthen the bond between people.

In essence, nurturing meaningful relationships requires intentionality, effort, and a genuine desire to connect with others on a deeper level. By actively listening, communicating openly, expressing gratitude, and engaging in shared experiences, individuals can cultivate strong bonds that enrich their lives and bring joy and fulfillment to both parties involved.

15

Recognizing the Impact of Relationships on Our Well-being

Our well-being is intricately tied to the quality of our relationships with others. Research has consistently shown that strong social connections can have a profound impact on our mental and physical health, contributing to lower levels of stress, increased happiness, and even a longer lifespan.

One key aspect of how relationships influence our well-being is through emotional support. Having a network of supportive friends, family members, or partners can provide us with a sense of security and comfort during challenging times. Knowing that we have someone to turn to for advice, encouragement, or simply a listening ear can significantly reduce feelings of loneliness and isolation.

In addition to emotional support, relationships also play a crucial role in promoting positive behaviors and habits. When we surround ourselves with individuals who prioritize health and well-being, we are more likely to adopt similar practices. Whether it's exercising together, cooking nutritious meals as a group, or engaging in mindfulness activities, shared experiences can motivate us to take better care of ourselves.

Furthermore, strong relationships can enhance our sense of purpose and belonging. Feeling connected to others and being part of a community fosters a sense of identity and meaning in our lives. This sense of belonging can boost self-esteem, confidence, and overall life satisfaction.

Recognizing the impact of relationships on our well-being underscores the importance of investing time and effort into nurturing meaningful connections. By prioritizing healthy relationships and surrounding ourselves with supportive individuals who uplift us, we not only enhance our own well-being but also contribute positively to the well-being of those around us.

Chapter 4:
Finding Value in Experiences

The Power of Memorable Experiences

Memorable experiences hold a unique power in shaping our perceptions, emotions, and memories. These experiences have the ability to leave a lasting impact on our lives, influencing how we view the world around us and the relationships we form with others.

One key aspect of memorable experiences is their ability to evoke strong emotions and feelings. Whether it's a thrilling adventure, a heartwarming moment with loved ones, or a significant achievement, these experiences elicit joy, excitement, gratitude, or even sadness. The intensity of these emotions creates vivid memories that stay with us long after the experience has passed.

Moreover, memorable experiences often serve as milestones in our personal growth and development. They challenge us to step out of our comfort zones, confront fears, or embrace new opportunities. By pushing boundaries and expanding our horizons, these experiences contribute to our sense of self-discovery and resilience.

In addition to personal growth, memorable experiences also play a crucial role in strengthening bonds with others. Shared adventures or meaningful moments create connections based on mutual understanding and shared memories. These shared experiences foster empathy, trust, and camaraderie among individuals, deepening the relationships we have with friends, family, or partners.

Furthermore, memorable experiences can act as sources of inspiration and motivation in times of difficulty or uncertainty. Reflecting on past achievements or cherished moments can provide reassurance and confidence during challenging situations. These memories serve as reminders of our capabilities and strengths, encouraging us to persevere through obstacles.

In essence, the power of memorable experiences lies in their ability to enrich our lives with meaning, emotion, and connection. By embracing new adventures, cherishing special moments with loved ones, and reflecting on past achievements, we can cultivate a sense of gratitude for the richness that these experiences bring into our lives.

19

Seeking Meaningful and Fulfilling Experiences

Seeking meaningful and fulfilling experiences is a fundamental aspect of human nature, as it allows individuals to find purpose, satisfaction, and joy in their lives. These experiences go beyond mere enjoyment or entertainment; they provide a deeper sense of fulfillment that resonates with one's values, beliefs, and aspirations.

Self-Reflection: Meaningful experiences often require introspection and self- awareness. By reflecting on personal values, goals, and desires, individuals can identify the types of experiences that align with their authentic selves. This self-awareness guides them towards activities and relationships that bring genuine fulfillment.

Connection to Others: Meaningful experiences are often intertwined with relationships and connections with others. Whether it's sharing a passion with like-minded individuals or supporting loved ones through challenging times, these interactions contribute to a sense of belonging and purpose. Building strong connections enhances the richness of experiences and fosters a deeper appreciation for life.

Growth and Development: Seeking meaningful experiences involves stepping out of comfort zones and embracing challenges that promote personal growth. These experiences push individuals to learn new skills, overcome obstacles, and expand their perspectives. Through this process of growth, individuals gain confidence, resilience, and a greater understanding of themselves.

Furthermore, seeking meaningful experiences requires openness to new possibilities and a willingness to explore unfamiliar territories. By embracing novelty and diversity in experiences, individuals can broaden their horizons, cultivate curiosity, and enrich their lives with diverse perspectives.

In essence, seeking meaningful and fulfilling experiences is about living intentionally, pursuing activities that resonate with one's values and aspirations while fostering personal growth, connection with others, and a deep sense of purpose.

Embracing the Journey Over the Destination

Embracing the journey over the destination is a mindset that emphasizes the process and experiences encountered along the way rather than solely focusing on reaching a specific goal or endpoint. This approach encourages individuals to appreciate each step of their journey, savoring the moments, lessons, and growth opportunities that arise throughout the process.

Living in the Present: By prioritizing the journey, individuals are more inclined to live in the present moment, fully immersing themselves in their experiences without being fixated on future outcomes. This mindfulness allows for a deeper connection with oneself and one's surroundings, fostering a sense of gratitude and awareness.

Cultivating Resilience: Embracing the journey involves navigating through challenges, setbacks, and uncertainties that inevitably arise. By viewing these obstacles as integral parts of personal growth and development, individuals can cultivate resilience, adaptability, and perseverance. Each hurdle becomes an opportunity for learning and self-improvement.

Fostering Creativity: The journey often presents unexpected twists, turns, and opportunities for exploration. By embracing uncertainty and spontaneity, individuals can tap into their creativity, problem-solving skills, and resourcefulness. This openness to new possibilities sparks innovation and ingenuity along the way.

Moreover, embracing the journey over the destination encourages individuals to adopt a flexible mindset that embraces change and adaptation. Rather than rigidly adhering to a predetermined path or outcome, this approach allows for fluidity and evolution based on new insights and experiences gained during the journey.

In essence, valuing the journey over the destination enriches one's life with depth, meaning, and fulfillment by emphasizing personal growth, resilience-building, creativity cultivation, mindfulness practice, and adaptability in navigating life's twists and turns.

Chapter 5:
Self-Worth and Personal Beliefs

Understanding Self-Value and Self-Esteem

Self-value and self-esteem are foundational aspects of an individual's sense of worth and identity. Understanding these concepts is crucial for personal growth, emotional well-being, and healthy relationships with oneself and others.

Self-value refers to the intrinsic worth that individuals attribute to themselves, independent of external factors such as achievements or validation from others. It involves recognizing one's inherent dignity, uniqueness, and deservingness of respect and care. Cultivating self- value requires self-compassion, acceptance of imperfections, and acknowledgment of personal strengths.

In contrast, self-esteem pertains to the evaluation of one's abilities, qualities, and overall self-worth based on internal beliefs and perceptions. It encompasses feelings of confidence, competence, and self-assurance in various domains of life. Building healthy self-esteem involves challenging negative self-talk, setting realistic goals, celebrating achievements, and fostering a positive self-image.

Understanding self-value and self-esteem involves introspection, reflection on past experiences, and awareness of how internal beliefs shape thoughts and behaviors. By exploring the origins of negative beliefs or insecurities, individuals can work towards reframing their perspectives, developing a more compassionate relationship with themselves.

Moreover, recognizing the interconnectedness between self-value and self-esteem is essential for holistic personal development. While self-value lays the foundation for a sense of inherent worthiness regardless of external circumstances, nurturing positive self-esteem reinforces feelings of competence and confidence in navigating life's challenges.

In essence, understanding self-value and self-esteem is about cultivating a deep sense of respect for oneself while also building confidence in one's abilities and worthiness. By embracing these concepts with compassion and authenticity, individuals can foster a strong sense of identity grounded in resilience, positivity, and inner strength.

Challenging Limiting Beliefs About Our Worth

Challenging limiting beliefs about our worth is a crucial step in fostering a healthy sense of self-value and self-esteem. These beliefs often stem from past experiences, societal norms, or comparisons with others, leading individuals to underestimate their inherent worth and potential.

To challenge these limiting beliefs effectively, individuals must first identify and acknowledge them. This process involves introspection, reflection on recurring negative thoughts or patterns, and recognizing the impact of these beliefs on one's self-perception and behavior.

Once identified, it is essential to question the validity of these beliefs. Are they based on objective evidence or distorted perceptions? By examining the origins and rationale behind these beliefs, individuals can begin to challenge their accuracy and replace them with more empowering narratives.

Practicing self-compassion is another key aspect of challenging limiting beliefs about worth. It involves treating oneself with kindness, understanding, and acceptance, especially when confronting insecurities or doubts. By cultivating a compassionate inner dialogue, individuals can counteract negative self-talk and build a more positive self-image.

Setting realistic goals and celebrating achievements are also effective strategies for challenging limiting beliefs. By acknowledging personal strengths, accomplishments, and progress towards growth, individuals can boost their confidence and reinforce a sense of worthiness.

Moreover, seeking support from trusted friends, family members, or mental health professionals can provide valuable perspectives and encouragement in challenging limiting beliefs. Surrounding oneself with positive influences who affirm one's value and potential can help reshape internal narratives and foster a stronger sense of self-worth.

In essence, challenging limiting beliefs about our worth requires courage, introspection, self-compassion, goal-setting, celebration of achievements, and seeking support when needed. By actively engaging in this process, individuals can gradually dismantle negative perceptions about themselves and cultivate a deeper appreciation for their inherent worthiness.

Cultivating a Positive Sense of Self-Worth

Cultivating a positive sense of self-worth is essential for overall well-being and personal growth. It involves recognizing and appreciating one's own value, strengths, and uniqueness, regardless of external validation or comparison with others.

One key aspect of fostering self-worth is practicing self-acceptance. This involves embracing all aspects of oneself, including flaws and imperfections, without judgment or criticism. By acknowledging and accepting both strengths and weaknesses, individuals can develop a more balanced and realistic view of themselves.

Self-awareness plays a crucial role in cultivating self-worth. It involves understanding one's emotions, thoughts, beliefs, and behaviors, as well as how they influence self-perception. Through introspection and reflection, individuals can gain insight into their inner workings and make conscious choices that align with their values and goals.

Setting boundaries is another important component of building self-worth. By establishing clear boundaries in relationships, work environments, and personal life, individuals communicate their needs and values effectively. Respecting these boundaries reinforces a sense of self-respect and worthiness.

Practicing gratitude is a powerful tool for enhancing self-worth. By focusing on the positive aspects of life, expressing appreciation for blessings big and small, individuals can shift their perspective from lack to abundance. Gratitude fosters a sense of contentment and fulfillment that contributes to a positive self-image.

In conclusion, cultivating a positive sense of self-worth requires self-acceptance, self- awareness, setting boundaries, practicing gratitude, among other strategies. By actively engaging in these practices consistently over time, individuals can strengthen their belief in their inherent worthiness and lead more fulfilling lives.

Chapter 6:
Societal Influences on Perceptions of Value

Cultural Norms and Values

Cultural norms and values play a significant role in shaping individuals' perceptions of value, self-worth, and identity. These societal influences provide a framework within which individuals navigate their beliefs, behaviors, and relationships with others.

One key aspect of cultural norms is the emphasis placed on collectivism versus individualism. In collectivist cultures, such as many Asian societies, the community's well-being and harmony are prioritized over individual achievements. This can impact how individuals perceive their worth, as success may be measured not only by personal accomplishments but also by contributions to the group.

Conversely, individualistic cultures like those in Western societies often prioritize personal autonomy, self-expression, and achievement. In these contexts, self-worth may be closely tied to individual accomplishments, career success, or material wealth. The pressure to excel on a personal level can influence how individuals view themselves and their value within society.

Cultural norms also shape gender roles and expectations, influencing perceptions of value based on traditional stereotypes. For example, in some cultures, men may be valued for their strength, leadership abilities, or financial success, while women are expected to prioritize caregiving roles or domestic responsibilities. These ingrained beliefs can impact individuals' self-esteem and sense of worth based on societal standards.

Moreover, cultural values around beauty standards, body image ideals, and social status can significantly impact how individuals perceive their own worth. Media representations of beauty often perpetuate unrealistic standards that can lead to feelings of inadequacy or low self-esteem among those who do not conform to these ideals.

In conclusion, cultural norms and values exert a powerful influence on individuals' perceptions of value and self-worth. By understanding the societal context in which these beliefs are formed and challenging limiting stereotypes or expectations imposed by culture, individuals can cultivate a more authentic sense of worthiness that aligns with their true selves.

Media Influence on Our Perception of Worth

The media plays a crucial role in shaping our perceptions of worth by influencing the values, beliefs, and ideals we internalize. Through various forms of media such as television, movies, magazines, and social media platforms, individuals are constantly bombarded with messages that dictate what is considered valuable or desirable in society.

One significant way in which the media impacts our perception of worth is through the portrayal of beauty standards. Advertisements and entertainment industries often promote unrealistic ideals of beauty that can lead to feelings of inadequacy among individuals who do not conform to these standards. This can result in low self-esteem and a distorted sense of self-worth as people strive to attain an unattainable image.

Moreover, the media also influences our perception of worth through its representation of success and wealth. Television shows and movies often glamorize material possessions, luxury lifestyles, and career achievements as markers of success. This can create a culture where individuals equate their value with their financial status or professional accomplishments, leading to a constant pursuit of external validation.

Social media platforms further exacerbate this phenomenon by showcasing curated versions of people's lives that emphasize achievements, experiences, and possessions. The pressure to present an idealized version of oneself online can contribute to feelings of inadequacy and comparison with others, further impacting one's sense of self-worth.

In conclusion, the media exerts a powerful influence on our perceptions of worth by shaping our ideals around beauty, success, and wealth. By being mindful consumers of media content and critically analyzing the messages we are exposed to, individuals can challenge societal norms and cultivate a more authentic sense of self-worth that is not solely based on external factors.

Examining Societal Expectations and Their Impact on Personal Worth

Societal expectations play a significant role in shaping individuals' perceptions of their own worth. From a young age, people are exposed to societal norms and standards that dictate what is considered valuable or desirable in various aspects of life, including appearance, career success, relationships, and personal achievements.

One key aspect of societal expectations is the pressure to conform to specific beauty standards. These standards are often perpetuated by media representations of idealized beauty, leading individuals to compare themselves to these unrealistic images. As a result, many people may develop feelings of inadequacy or low self-esteem if they do not meet these beauty ideals, impacting their sense of personal worth.

Moreover, societal expectations regarding success and achievement can also influence how individuals perceive their own value. In a culture that glorifies material wealth and professional accomplishments as markers of success, individuals may feel pressured to constantly strive for external validation through their careers or financial status. This can create a cycle of seeking approval from others rather than valuing oneself intrinsically.

Additionally, societal expectations around relationships and social status can impact personal worth. The pressure to conform to certain relationship norms or social hierarchies can lead individuals to base their self-worth on external factors such as the approval of others or the perceived status of their relationships. This can result in feelings of insecurity or unworthiness if one does not meet these societal expectations.

In conclusion, examining societal expectations and their impact on personal worth highlights the importance of recognizing and challenging these norms. By fostering a sense of self-worth that is independent of external validation and societal pressures, individuals can cultivate a more authentic and resilient sense of value based on their intrinsic qualities and unique attributes.

Chapter 7:
Individual Experiences Shaping Perceptions of Value

How Personal Experiences Shape Our Definitions of Preciousness

Personal experiences play a crucial role in shaping our definitions of preciousness and value. These experiences can range from significant life events to everyday interactions, all of which contribute to how we perceive the worth of people, objects, or concepts in our lives.

One way personal experiences influence our definitions of preciousness is through emotional connections. For example, an individual may attach sentimental value to a family heirloom because it reminds them of cherished memories with loved ones. This emotional bond enhances the perceived preciousness of the object beyond its material worth, highlighting the subjective nature of value perception.

Moreover, personal achievements and milestones can also shape our definitions of preciousness. Accomplishing a long-term goal or overcoming a challenging obstacle can imbue a sense of pride and significance to that particular achievement, elevating its value in our eyes. These personal triumphs become markers of self-worth and contribute to how we define what is truly valuable in our lives.

Additionally, negative experiences such as loss or failure can also impact how we perceive preciousness. Losing something or someone dear to us can highlight the fragility and impermanence of life, leading us to reevaluate what truly matters and holds value in our existence. These moments of vulnerability often prompt introspection and a deeper appreciation for the things we hold dear.

In conclusion, personal experiences are powerful influencers in shaping our definitions of preciousness. By reflecting on the emotions, achievements, and challenges that have marked our journey through life, we gain insight into what holds true value for us as individuals. These reflections help us cultivate a more nuanced understanding of what is truly precious and meaningful in our lives beyond external standards or societal expectations.

Overcoming Trauma and Reevaluating Priorities

Overcoming trauma is a transformative experience that can profoundly impact how individuals perceive value and prioritize aspects of their lives. Trauma, whether stemming from personal loss, abuse, or other distressing events, can shatter one's sense of security and stability, leading to a reevaluation of what truly matters.

Individuals who have navigated through traumatic experiences often develop a heightened appreciation for resilience and inner strength. The process of overcoming trauma requires immense courage and perseverance, highlighting the intrinsic value of mental fortitude and emotional resilience in the face of adversity. This newfound understanding of personal strength can reshape priorities, emphasizing the importance of self-care, mental well-being, and relationships over material possessions or societal expectations.

Moreover, overcoming trauma can foster a deeper sense of empathy and compassion towards others who may be facing similar challenges. Individuals who have triumphed over their own traumas often become advocates for mental health awareness or support systems for those in need. This shift towards prioritizing human connection and emotional support underscores the significance of empathy and solidarity in shaping perceptions of value beyond individual achievements or material wealth.

In essence, overcoming trauma serves as a catalyst for profound introspection and reevaluation of priorities. It prompts individuals to reassess their values, beliefs, and goals in light of their experiences, leading to a more authentic alignment between personal aspirations and what truly holds meaning in their lives. By confronting past traumas with courage and resilience, individuals can cultivate a deeper understanding of their own worth and the intrinsic value inherent in human connection and emotional well-being.

Learning from Past Mistakes to Redefine What is Truly Valuable

Learning from past mistakes is a crucial aspect of personal growth and development, shaping individuals' perceptions of value and priorities. Mistakes, whether in relationships, career choices, or financial decisions, offer valuable lessons that can lead to a reevaluation of what holds true significance in one's life.

When individuals reflect on their past errors and missteps, they gain insights into their values, beliefs, and aspirations. By acknowledging where they went wrong and understanding the consequences of their actions, individuals can redefine what truly matters to them. This process of introspection allows for a deeper understanding of personal values and the importance of aligning actions with those values.

Moreover, learning from past mistakes fosters resilience and adaptability in individuals. By confronting failures head-on and extracting lessons from them, individuals develop a sense of perseverance and determination that can guide them towards making more informed decisions in the future. This resilience becomes a valuable asset in navigating challenges and setbacks while staying true to one's core values.

Furthermore, redefining what is truly valuable after learning from past mistakes often involves prioritizing experiences over material possessions. Individuals may realize that lasting fulfillment comes from meaningful connections, personal growth, and experiences that enrich their lives rather than accumulating wealth or status symbols. This shift towards valuing intangible aspects of life highlights the transformative power of self-reflection and learning from past errors.

In essence, by embracing the lessons learned from past mistakes, individuals can redefine their perceptions of value by prioritizing authenticity, personal growth, and meaningful experiences over superficial markers of success. This journey towards reevaluating what holds true significance leads to a more fulfilling and purpose-driven life guided by intrinsic values rather than external expectations.

Chapter 8:
Exploring Human Emotions and Psychology

The Role of Emotions in Determining Value

Emotions play a significant role in determining the value we assign to people, objects, and concepts in our lives. Unlike rational assessments based solely on objective criteria, emotions add a layer of subjectivity that can greatly influence our perceptions of worth.

One key aspect of how emotions shape value is through the attachment of sentimental significance. For example, an individual may treasure a simple trinket not for its material worth but because it was a gift from a loved one, evoking feelings of love and connection. This emotional bond elevates the perceived value of the object beyond its physical attributes, highlighting the subjective nature of value determination.

Moreover, emotions can also impact how we prioritize certain aspects of our lives. For instance, the joy and fulfillment derived from spending time with family or pursuing a passion project can lead us to assign greater value to these experiences over material possessions or societal achievements. Emotions guide us towards what truly matters to us on a personal level, shaping our values and priorities accordingly.

Furthermore, negative emotions such as fear or regret can also influence how we perceive value. A past failure or loss may prompt us to reevaluate our choices and priorities, leading to a shift in what we consider valuable in life. These moments of introspection driven by negative emotions can be catalysts for personal growth and transformation as we realign our values with our emotional needs and aspirations.

In conclusion, emotions are powerful drivers in determining value as they provide depth and meaning to our assessments beyond mere logic or reason. By acknowledging and understanding the role of emotions in shaping our perceptions of worth, we gain insight into what truly holds significance in our lives and how these emotional connections contribute to our sense of fulfillment and happiness.

Psychological Factors Influencing Perceptions of Worth

Our perceptions of worth are not solely determined by rational assessments but are heavily influenced by psychological factors that shape how we assign value to people, objects, and concepts in our lives. Understanding these psychological influences can provide insight into the complexities of human behavior and decision-making.

One significant psychological factor that impacts perceptions of worth is self-esteem. Individuals with high self-esteem tend to value themselves more positively, leading them to assign greater worth to their own achievements, relationships, and possessions. On the other hand, individuals with low self-esteem may struggle to recognize their own value, resulting in a tendency to downplay their accomplishments or seek validation from external sources.

Moreover, cognitive biases play a crucial role in shaping perceptions of worth. Confirmation bias, for example, can lead individuals to selectively interpret information that aligns with their pre-existing beliefs or values, influencing how they assess the worth of different ideas or perspectives. Similarly, anchoring bias can cause individuals to fixate on initial impressions or values when making judgments about the worth of something, potentially overlooking relevant information that could alter their perception.

In addition to individual factors like self-esteem and cognitive biases, social influences also play a significant role in determining perceptions of worth. Social comparison theory suggests that individuals evaluate their own worth based on comparisons with others in similar situations or contexts. This comparison process can lead to feelings of inferiority or superiority depending on how one perceives themselves relative to others, ultimately impacting their sense of self- worth.

By recognizing the intricate interplay between psychological factors such as self-esteem, cognitive biases, and social influences in shaping perceptions of worth, we gain a deeper understanding of why individuals assign different values to various aspects of their lives. These insights highlight the complex nature of human psychology and emphasize the importance of considering these factors when exploring the dynamics of value determination. 43

Uncovering the Complexities of Human Emotions

Human emotions are a fundamental aspect of our psychological makeup, influencing our thoughts, behaviors, and interactions with the world around us. While emotions are often categorized into basic categories like happiness, sadness, anger, fear, and disgust, the complexities of human emotions go far beyond these simplistic labels.

One key aspect of human emotions is their multifaceted nature. Emotions are not isolated experiences but rather intricate blends of various feelings that can be influenced by a myriad of factors such as past experiences, cultural norms, and individual differences. For example, a person may experience a mix of joy and anxiety when faced with a new opportunity, highlighting the nuanced interplay between different emotional states.

Furthermore, emotions are dynamic and ever-changing. They can fluctuate rapidly in response to external stimuli or internal thoughts, leading to a wide range of emotional states within a short period. This fluidity in emotional experiences underscores the complexity of human emotions and challenges the notion of static emotional states.

In addition to their complexity and dynamism, human emotions also play a crucial role in shaping our perceptions and decision-making processes. Emotions can color our interpretations of events, influence our judgments about others, and guide our choices in various situations. Understanding the intricate ways in which emotions impact our cognitive processes is essential for gaining insight into human behavior and psychology.

By delving deeper into the complexities of human emotions, we uncover a rich tapestry of feelings that shape our everyday experiences and interactions. Exploring the nuances of emotional experiences can provide valuable insights into the intricacies of human psychology and offer a deeper understanding of what drives our thoughts, actions, and relationships.

45

Chapter 9:
Reflecting on What Truly Matters

Evaluating Priorities and Perspectives

When it comes to evaluating priorities and perspectives, individuals are often faced with the challenge of determining what truly matters in their lives. This process involves reflecting on personal values, beliefs, and goals to make informed decisions about where to allocate time, energy, and resources.

One key aspect of evaluating priorities is understanding the role of emotions in shaping our perceptions of value. Emotions can influence how we prioritize certain aspects of our lives by guiding us towards what brings us joy, fulfillment, and meaning. For example, the happiness derived from spending quality time with loved ones may lead individuals to prioritize relationships over material possessions or career achievements.

Moreover, perspectives play a crucial role in determining priorities as they shape how individuals perceive the world around them. Different perspectives can lead to varying assessments of worth and significance, highlighting the subjective nature of value determination. By considering diverse viewpoints and challenging preconceived notions, individuals can gain a more holistic understanding of what truly matters to them.

Furthermore, evaluating priorities involves introspection and self-reflection to align actions with core values and long-term goals. By clarifying personal values and identifying overarching objectives, individuals can make intentional choices that resonate with their authentic selves. This process requires honesty, vulnerability, and a willingness to confront difficult truths about one's desires and aspirations.

In conclusion, evaluating priorities and perspectives is a multifaceted process that requires individuals to delve deep into their emotions, beliefs, and aspirations. By acknowledging the influence of emotions on value determination and considering diverse perspectives when setting priorities, individuals can cultivate a sense of purpose, fulfillment, and alignment with what truly matters in their lives.

Identifying the Core Values that Bring Meaning to Life

Identifying core values is a crucial step in understanding what truly matters in life. These values serve as guiding principles that shape our decisions, actions, and overall sense of purpose. By identifying and prioritizing these core values, individuals can align their lives with what brings them fulfillment and meaning.

One key aspect of identifying core values is introspection. This process involves reflecting on past experiences, beliefs, and aspirations to uncover the underlying principles that drive our behavior. For example, someone who values honesty may prioritize transparency in their relationships and decision-making processes.

Moreover, core values often stem from deeply held beliefs about what is important and meaningful. These beliefs can be influenced by cultural background, personal experiences, or significant life events. By examining the origins of our core values, we can gain a deeper understanding of why certain principles hold significance for us.

Furthermore, identifying core values requires a willingness to prioritize authenticity over external expectations. In a world where societal norms and pressures can influence our choices, staying true to our core values can be challenging but ultimately rewarding. By staying aligned with our authentic selves, we can lead more fulfilling lives that are grounded in what truly matters to us.

In conclusion, identifying core values is an essential part of living a purposeful and meaningful life. By delving into our beliefs, experiences, and aspirations, we can uncover the guiding principles that shape our existence. Through introspection and authenticity, we can align our actions with what truly matters to us and cultivate a sense of fulfillment that transcends external validation.

Embracing Gratitude for the Precious Moments in Life

Embracing gratitude for the precious moments in life is a transformative practice that allows individuals to appreciate the beauty and significance of everyday experiences. By cultivating a sense of gratitude, individuals can shift their focus from what they lack to what they have, fostering a mindset of abundance and contentment.

Gratitude serves as a powerful tool for enhancing overall well-being and mental health. Research has shown that practicing gratitude can lead to increased levels of happiness, improved relationships, and reduced stress levels. By acknowledging and expressing gratitude for the small joys in life, individuals can cultivate a positive outlook and resilience in the face of challenges.

Moreover, embracing gratitude for the precious moments in life encourages mindfulness and presence. When individuals take the time to reflect on and savor moments of joy, love, or connection, they become more attuned to the present moment. This heightened awareness allows them to fully experience and cherish each moment as it unfolds, leading to a deeper sense of fulfillment and meaning.

Gratitude also fosters a sense of interconnectedness with others and the world around us. By recognizing and appreciating the contributions of others to our lives, we strengthen our relationships and build a sense of community. This interconnectedness reminds us that we are part of something greater than ourselves, instilling a sense of purpose and belonging.

In conclusion, embracing gratitude for the precious moments in life is an essential practice for living a fulfilling and meaningful existence. By cultivating gratitude, individuals can enhance their well-being, foster mindfulness, strengthen relationships, and deepen their connection to the world around them. Through this practice, individuals can find joy in even the simplest moments and truly appreciate all that life has to offer.

Chapter 10:
Cherishing the Priceless Treasures

Appreciating Connections and Relationships

Connections and relationships form the foundation of our lives, shaping our experiences, emotions, and sense of belonging. By appreciating these connections, individuals can cultivate a deeper understanding of themselves and others, fostering empathy, compassion, and mutual support.

One key aspect of appreciating connections is recognizing the impact that relationships have on our well-being. Research has shown that strong social connections are linked to increased happiness, reduced stress levels, and improved overall health. By valuing the people in our lives and nurturing meaningful relationships, we can enhance our quality of life and build a support system that sustains us through challenges.

Moreover, appreciating connections involves acknowledging the diversity of relationships we encounter. From family bonds to friendships to professional networks, each connection offers unique perspectives, insights, and opportunities for growth. By embracing this diversity and learning from different interactions, individuals can broaden their horizons and develop a richer understanding of the world around them.

Furthermore, appreciating connections requires active engagement and communication. Building strong relationships takes effort, time, and genuine interest in others' well-being. By listening attentively, expressing gratitude, and offering support when needed, individuals can strengthen their connections and create lasting bonds based on trust and respect.

In conclusion, appreciating connections and relationships is essential for leading a fulfilling life enriched by love, support, and shared experiences. By valuing the people in our lives, embracing diversity in relationships, and actively engaging with others, individuals can foster deep connections that bring joy, meaning, and a sense of belonging to their journey.

Nurturing Memories and Creating Lasting Legacies

Memories hold a special place in our hearts, serving as the threads that weave together the tapestry of our lives. Nurturing these memories and creating lasting legacies is not only a way to honor our past but also a means to shape our future.

One key aspect of nurturing memories is the act of reflection. By taking the time to reminisce about significant moments, both joyful and challenging, individuals can gain valuable insights into their personal growth and development. Reflecting on past experiences allows us to appreciate how far we have come, learn from our mistakes, and cherish the lessons learned along the way.

Moreover, creating lasting legacies involves more than just preserving memories; it entails actively shaping the narrative of our lives for future generations. Whether through storytelling, documenting family history, or passing down traditions, individuals can leave behind a legacy that transcends time and connects generations to come.

Furthermore, nurturing memories and creating lasting legacies require intentional actions. From capturing precious moments through photographs or journals to sharing stories with loved ones, every effort contributes to preserving the essence of who we are and what we stand for. These actions not only strengthen familial bonds but also instill a sense of belonging and continuity within our communities.

In conclusion, by nurturing memories and creating lasting legacies, individuals can ensure that their stories endure beyond their lifetime. These cherished treasures serve as a testament to the richness of human experience and the enduring power of love, resilience, and connection across generations.

Finding Joy in Simple Pleasures

Amidst the hustle and bustle of modern life, finding joy in simple pleasures is a crucial aspect of cherishing the priceless treasures that enrich our existence. These simple pleasures are often overlooked in the pursuit of grand achievements or material possessions, yet they hold the power to bring profound happiness and contentment.

One key element of finding joy in simple pleasures is cultivating mindfulness and presence in everyday moments. By slowing down and savoring the small joys that surround us, such as a warm cup of tea on a rainy day or a heartfelt conversation with a loved one, we can tap into a wellspring of happiness that transcends external circumstances.

Moreover, embracing gratitude plays a vital role in appreciating the beauty of simple pleasures. When we express gratitude for the little things that bring us joy – whether it's a beautiful sunset or a kind gesture from a stranger – we cultivate a sense of abundance and fulfillment that enhances our overall well-being.

In addition, fostering connections with nature can be a powerful source of joy and tranquility. Spending time outdoors, breathing in fresh air, and immersing ourselves in the natural world can provide solace and rejuvenation, reminding us of the beauty and wonder that surrounds us every day.

Ultimately, finding joy in simple pleasures is not about extravagant experiences or material wealth; it is about embracing the richness of life's small moments and allowing them to nourish our souls. By prioritizing these simple pleasures and relishing their inherent beauty, we can cultivate a deep sense of contentment and gratitude that enriches our lives immeasurably.

Chapter 11:
Embracing the Power of Mindfulness
Cultivating Mindfulness in Everyday Life

Mindfulness is a powerful practice that involves being fully present and aware of one's thoughts, feelings, sensations, and surroundings. Cultivating mindfulness in everyday life can have profound benefits for mental well-being, emotional regulation, and overall quality of life.

One key aspect of cultivating mindfulness is developing a non-judgmental awareness of the present moment. By observing thoughts and emotions without attaching labels or criticisms, individuals can cultivate a sense of acceptance and inner peace. This practice allows for greater clarity of mind and the ability to respond to situations with intention rather than reacting impulsively.

Moreover, integrating mindfulness into daily routines can help individuals manage stress more effectively. By taking moments throughout the day to pause, breathe, and center oneself in the present moment, individuals can reduce anxiety levels, improve focus, and enhance resilience in the face of challenges.

In addition to personal well-being, cultivating mindfulness can also deepen connections with others. By practicing active listening, empathy, and presence in interactions with loved ones or colleagues, individuals can foster deeper relationships built on understanding and compassion. This mindful approach to communication enhances mutual respect and strengthens bonds based on authenticity and genuine connection.

Furthermore, incorporating mindfulness practices such as meditation or body scans into daily rituals can promote self-awareness and emotional regulation. These practices allow individuals to tune into their physical sensations, emotions, and thoughts with curiosity and kindness. By developing this heightened awareness of internal experiences, individuals can navigate life's ups and downs with greater equanimity and resilience.

In conclusion, cultivating mindfulness in everyday life is a transformative practice that can enhance mental clarity, emotional well-being, interpersonal relationships, and overall quality of life. By embracing the power of mindfulness through intentional awareness and presence in each moment, individuals can cultivate a deep sense of peace, resilience, and fulfillment in their daily experiences.

The Benefits of Practicing Mindfulness

Practicing mindfulness offers a myriad of benefits that extend beyond individual well-being to encompass various aspects of life. By cultivating intentional awareness and presence in each moment, individuals can experience transformative effects on their mental, emotional, and relational dimensions.

Enhanced Mental Clarity: Mindfulness practice fosters a clear and focused mind by training individuals to observe their thoughts without judgment. This heightened awareness allows for better decision-making, problem-solving, and cognitive functioning.

Improved Emotional Well-Being: By developing a non-judgmental acceptance of emotions and sensations, mindfulness helps individuals regulate their emotional responses effectively. This leads to reduced stress levels, increased emotional resilience, and a greater sense of inner peace.

Strengthened Interpersonal Relationships: Mindful communication promotes deeper connections with others through active listening, empathy, and presence. By being fully engaged in interactions without distractions or preconceptions, individuals can foster authentic relationships built on understanding and compassion.

Promotion of Self-Awareness: Mindfulness practices such as meditation or body scans enable individuals to tune into their internal experiences with curiosity and kindness. This heightened self-awareness enhances emotional regulation, self-reflection, and personal growth.

The benefits of practicing mindfulness are not limited to individual well-being but also extend to societal impacts. Research has shown that communities with higher levels of mindfulness exhibit lower rates of conflict, improved cooperation, and enhanced social cohesion. By embracing the power of mindfulness collectively, societies can cultivate environments that prioritize empathy, understanding, and mutual respect.

In conclusion, the benefits of practicing mindfulness are far-reaching and profound. By integrating mindful awareness into daily routines and interactions, individuals can experience enhanced mental clarity, emotional well-being, interpersonal relationships, self-awareness, and contribute positively to broader societal dynamics.

Applying Mindfulness to Enhance Appreciation and Value

Applying mindfulness to enhance appreciation and value involves cultivating a deep sense of gratitude and recognition for the present moment, experiences, and relationships. By practicing intentional awareness and presence, individuals can elevate their perception of everyday occurrences and interactions, leading to a profound shift in how they engage with the world around them.

Cultivating Gratitude: Mindfulness encourages individuals to acknowledge and appreciate the small moments of joy, beauty, and kindness that often go unnoticed in the hustle of daily life. By pausing to savor these moments with gratitude, individuals can cultivate a positive outlook and a deeper sense of fulfillment.

Recognizing Value: Through mindfulness practices such as mindful eating or walking meditation, individuals can develop a heightened awareness of the intrinsic value present in each experience. This increased sensitivity allows for a more profound connection to one's surroundings, fostering a sense of reverence for life's inherent richness.

Fostering Meaningful Connections: By approaching interactions with mindfulness, individuals can deepen their relationships by truly listening, empathizing, and engaging authentically. This level of presence fosters mutual understanding and respect, enhancing the quality of connections and creating lasting bonds based on shared values.

By applying mindfulness to enhance appreciation and value in daily life, individuals can transform mundane routines into opportunities for growth, connection, and fulfillment. This intentional practice not only enriches personal well-being but also contributes positively to broader societal dynamics by promoting empathy, compassion, and gratitude within communities.

In conclusion, integrating mindfulness into daily practices allows individuals to elevate their experiences by fostering gratitude, recognizing intrinsic value in each moment, and nurturing meaningful connections. By embracing this approach wholeheartedly, individuals can unlock a deeper sense of appreciation for life's richness while contributing positively to their own well- being and that of those around them.

-To God Be The Glory-